Gabriella's Haircut

Gabriella's Haircut

by

Audrey Le Roy

Gabriella's Haircut/Audrey Le Roy ISBN: 979-8-218-00573-3

Front cover design: Soosan Joon
Book layout and back cover design: Indigo Design
Back cover photo credit: Eli Lefkowitz

Dedication

for my parents Hedy & George,

and for Gabriella

"My daughter's good friend Audrey asked me to do some drawings for a book she was writing about her family during World War II. Being 90 years old I hesitated at first because I had not done any art work in over 30 years. Then I sat down and read her book. Tears came to my eyes and a strong, loving connection to a dear little girl named Gabriella developed. I felt I knew her, having been born just five years before her. Images of the sweet little girl filled my head and heart. I drew sketches of her over and over until I felt 'this is her.'

Dance little Gabriella, dance."

Phyllis Riforgiato

Prologue
1938

There are no photographs of young Gabriella.

A family portrait was taken in 1938, but she was little at the time, and the photographer and his strange camera frightened her.

Happy and easygoing at the start, she began to cry when the photographer emerged from under the black cloth hood connected to his camera. The mysterious-looking camera equipment terrified her, and she was inconsolable. After several attempts, the family portrait was taken without her.

The photographer's wife distracted the little girl with a teddy bear as four brothers, ages six to thirteen, were arranged with their parents for a family portrait session.

Shortly after this incomplete family photograph was taken, Gabriella's parents mailed a copy of it to relatives in New York City.

dancing little girl

G abriella was a beautiful child with big blue eyes and long, blonde, wavy hair. She was born on the first day of July in 1935.

Her eyes were as blue as the sky on a perfect day, and her smile melted the hearts of the people in her small town. Tall for her age with long legs, she loved to dance.

Gabriella was her father's dancing little girl who brought joy to the entire family.

One of her mother's sweetest pleasures was washing Gabriella's silky blonde hair and then brushing it until it shined like glass. Every day, she braided a red ribbon into her daughter's long braid. Sometimes, after washing it, she would let Gabriella dance first while her hair dried, long and flowing free.

Gabriella's strands of long, blonde, wavy hair moved rhythmically as she danced for her father.

beautiful long hair

Decades after Gabriella was a young girl, Audrey was born on the 29th day of September.

Audrey also had beautiful long hair. She had the longest hair in her school, and people who didn't know her name would describe her as "the little girl with the long hair."

Audrey's father George loved his daughter's long hair, because it reminded him of his younger sister Gabriella. Audrey felt proud knowing that something of hers could bring him such happy memories. She loved to make her father smile.

George came from Hungary shortly after the end of World War II. He tried to keep the cheerful images of his little sister in his memory, but sometimes the bad memories clouded the happy ones. George would think back to joyful holiday memories lighting candles and singing songs with his family back in Europe. But he would get misty-eyed thinking about his parents and siblings.

Audrey sensed a deep sadness behind the twinkle in her father's blue eyes. Softly, she said, "Daddy, tell me about your life before you came to America."

He lowered his eyes and got quiet, choosing his words carefully. He didn't want Audrey and her two brothers to know about the horrors he has witnessed.

"I started a new life when I was twenty years old," he said, "and I celebrate the day I arrived in America as another birthday. With God's help, I came to this blessed land on September 16th, 1946. Today, I'm a proud American."

There was an old photograph on the wall of George with his parents and brothers, but his little sister Gabriella was not in it. Audrey wondered why.

"Tell me about Gabriella," Audrey begged.

❀　❀　❀　❀　❀　❀

four older brothers

The only girl in a family with four older brothers, Gabriella was eight years old enjoying a simple, happy life in the small northeastern Hungarian town of Nyirmada when her life suddenly changed.

Earlier generations of her family had lived in this town for centuries. Grave markers in the cemetery bearing her family name dated back 350 years.

Everyone in this friendly town knew each other. Some of the townspeople were Catholic, some Greek Orthodox, some Evangelical, and some Jewish. For hundreds of years, these families of different faiths lived together in peace and harmony.

Gabriella's Jewish family always observed the Sabbath, which was a pleasant and comforting routine for all of them. Gabriella loved to help her mother in the kitchen and welcomed any opportunity to lend a helping hand.

She watched as her mother kneaded the dough and then braided the challah bread, crossing and weaving the three sections over each other just as she braided Gabriella's long hair.

After the two loaves of challah were baked, they were placed on the table and covered with a white cloth napkin, waiting for blessings to be said before dinner. When the sun went down, Gabriella watched as her mother lit the candles on their beautiful silver candlesticks and silently said the Sabbath prayers. The evening ended with the family singing and laughing—a happy time for all of them.

The family lived in a modest stucco house with a wood shingled roof and a large backyard. There was a barn for their horses and cow along with a large chicken coop, which also housed their geese.

Every spring, the acacia trees lining the street bloomed and showed off their fuzzy pompom flowers with a soft, delicate fragrance that filled the neighborhood with sweetness.

This springtime—1944—was different.

war in Europe

As the war in Europe spread and the fires of war drew closer to Gabriella's Hungarian town, restrictions were applied to all Jewish families. One of them, called *Numerus Clausus* in Latin and meaning "closed number," restricted the number of Jewish children who could continue their advanced education, including university studies. Gabriella's mother had attended college in the early 1920s, a rare event for girls in those days. She had always encouraged her children to embrace continuing education and lifelong learning. So, the family had to find ways around these restrictions by hiring private tutors for all the children.

Gabriella once overheard her mother say, "We must do everything we can to teach the children."

At this point, the people in Gabriella's town were as accepting of their Jewish neighbors as they always had been, so the family's lives remained rooted in regular routines. After completing their daily studies, Gabriella's four brothers—aged twelve, sixteen, eighteen and nineteen—went outside to play soccer.

Young Gabriella often stood at the door waving to the boys and their friends as they walked away, kicking a soccer ball among them. But she often wondered, "Why can't my brothers and their friends go to school?"

She was too young to know what was going on in the world. Her parents kept their emotions out of view from their children. Instead, they showed them examples of happiness and gratitude as if an imaginary blanket of good thoughts could protectively wrap the family from the changing world around them.

Gabriella's youth and innocence were a pleasant distraction for the family and a source of amusement for all of them. Hearing her giggles provided a welcome relief at the end of each day. Her dancing and cheerful disposition raised the spirits of the entire family. If Gabriella saw her parents looking sad, she would try to make them happy with extra twirling and singing.

❀   ❀   ❀   ❀   ❀   ❀

false news stories

In 1944, political rallies were held in Hungary and the crowds were told lies, spreading awful, hateful viewpoints among the people. Propaganda films were shown in movie theaters and false news was spiraling outward toward the small towns and villages in northeastern Hungary.

The people in Gabriella's town had been isolated from what was happening in the rest of the world. They remained uninformed about the truth. Newspaper articles were carefully worded, and nothing was reported about the reality of what was happening in other parts of Europe.

But the outbreak of false news stories quickly and effectively led the people of Hungary to believe they would be better off if they banned Jewish people from living there altogether! They planned to relocate them to another country, possibly Madagascar, an island in the Indian Ocean off the southeast coast of Africa.

No one pushed back on this. Nobody asked questions. No one spoke up for the Jewish families.

Something had ignited hate in Gabriella's little town where people of all different faiths had lived together in peace and harmony for centuries. This was confusing to a child whose loving heart came naturally.

What motivated the people of Hungary to turn their backs on their Jewish friends?

relocation plan announced

A relocation plan was explained in simple terms: Jewish people would be taken to a work camp. The older people and the children would stay in the camp, while able-bodied people would work eight hours a day. It sounded like a plan that would keep families together, so Gabriella's parents tried to make the best of this situation.

Still, Gabriella wondered, "Why do they want the Jewish people to go away?" and "What will happen to our family?"

Although frightened, she didn't want to show her parents and her four brothers just how scared she was, so she kept her questions to herself. Instinctively, she knew her parents needed her to be brave. She thought, "I didn't do anything wrong. I didn't commit any crimes. I was born Jewish. That's all."

Gabriella's father—a proud Hungarian—had been a cavalry officer in the Austro-Hungarian Royal Army during the first World War. He said, "This relocation won't happen to us. The Hungarian government will protect us."

The family members wanted to believe this, even though they felt anxious about not knowing what would happen next. So, they lived normally as long as they could. The young girl continued to rely on her songs and dancing routines to bring pleasant distractions to the family. Every day, she told herself, "Be brave; tomorrow will be better."

Her gentle spirit sparkled around the madness surrounding them.

❋   ❋   ❋   ❋   ❋   ❋

new laws passed

A new law was passed that commanded all the Jewish people of Hungary to sew a yellow star onto their clothes. The star was to be worn on their overcoats, so they could be easily identified at all times.

Yellow was the color of cowardice. The purpose of the yellow star was to isolate and shame the person wearing it—in this case, the Jews of Hungary.

At first, their movement was curtailed, and travel was limited to the village borders. Then, suddenly without warning, they were ordered confined to their homes. Gabriella's parents were overwhelmed by the swiftly changing laws limiting the activities of all the Jewish people in their town.

One day, after walking into the kitchen and seeing her mother and father cry, Gabriella was filled with fear and a deep sadness. She wanted to make them happy again. But her songs and dances were no longer enough to ease their tremendous fear.

Big changes were coming for Gabriella's family. It was only a matter of time.

recalling sweet memories

Audrey always knew her parents were different. She didn't ask too many questions because she wanted to make their sadness go away. Asking questions might make them feel worse.

Holidays always brought back memories of family members who were gone. They were not occasions for questions or discussions about the past. And she knew the time would come when they would be ready to talk about that sadness. For now, she kept her questions to herself.

When George watched his wife brush their daughter's long hair, he recalled happy childhood memories of his mother washing Gabriella's long silky blonde hair and brushing it until it shined like glass. It brought back happy images of them in his mind.

Getting lost in the repetition of the brush strokes, he always insisted Audrey's hair be kept long because of those *sweet memories. She wore her hair in a long ponytail until it became so long, her mother neatly braided it into two beautiful braids.*

Like Gabriella, Audrey was the apple of her father's eye.

relocation process begins

Two soldiers on motorcycles came to Gabriella's town bearing the Nazi flag. The soldiers took over its police station peacefully. Not a single shot was fired.

It was late April 1944 and still cold outside when the Hungarian Royal Gendarmes came to Gabriella's house. The gendarmerie consisted of thousands of policemen who were responsible for enforcing the new laws across the country. The gendarmes themselves were stern, and their presence intimidated and frightened the townspeople. The uniform worn by the Hungarian Royal Gendarmes included a distinctive hat. Gabriella couldn't take her eyes off the large rooster feathers pinned on the left side of their hats.

She stood transfixed as the officers entered her house.

The gendarmes had come to make a list of items of value in their home. One had a pad of paper and wrote quickly as the others picked up and evaluated everything they found. Gabriella saw her father hand over his pocket watch and her mother's beautiful ring to the officers. She had so many questions in her head, but she knew this was not the time to speak. She stood quietly, staying close to her mother.

For now, she kept her questions to herself.

After the inventory of valuables was completed, the family received instructions for all the Jewish people to assemble in the village square. Families were directed to pack up only what they could carry on their backs.

Among the instructions was a requirement to arrive at the village square with a very short haircut. "Why do we need to cut off our hair?" Gabriella asked. Her mother calmly and gently explained that these were official commands by the gendarmes to benefit the family's health and safety on the trip. The gendarmes hinted at the possibility of unsanitary conditions during their travels to the work camp, and short hair would be easier to keep clean.

At that point, final preparations for their journey began.

❀ ❀ ❀ ❀ ❀ ❀

long wavy hair

A udrey's mother washed her daughter's long hair in the bathtub and carefully combed through the tangles before braiding the wet hair into two very long braids.

This mother-and-daughter routine provided hours of closeness between them. Each morning, Audrey shared school stories or just sat quietly together with her mother as her hair was brushed and braided.

As her twelfth birthday approached, Audrey's mother thought it was time for her daughter to learn how to wash and care for her own hair. But she knew all that long hair was too much for a beginner to handle. So, one day as she braided Audrey's hair, she announced, "You have to get a haircut."

Audrey resisted. She was proud she had the longest hair in her school and, best of all, it reminded her father of his little sister Gabriella. She twirled the end of her braid in her *fingers as she thought about what it would be like without having long hair, not yet aware of the story of Gabriella's haircut.*

She soon learned the truth.

❀ ❀ ❀ ❀ ❀ ❀

Gabriella's haircut

The night before the Jewish people had to report to the town square for relocation, the family packed and prepared for their journey. All evening, Gabriella's mother was feeling anxious about cutting her daughter's beautiful hair. She understood the instructions and the reason for the haircuts, and she realized she couldn't delay any longer. It had to be done that evening.

So, she lovingly and gently washed Gabriella's hair with tenderness like a mother washing a newborn baby. Then she brushed it until it shined like glass. The hair looked like a waterfall flowing past Gabriella's shoulders down to her waist. She smoothed the silky hair into a ponytail, then braided it, tying it with the red ribbon. Then she sat for what seemed like a long time admiring the beautiful shiny hair. Finally, with tears in her eyes, she picked up the scissors and slowly but gently cut off the braid.

When she was finished, she placed her daughter's beautiful hair on a white linen tablecloth and rolled it up with her treasured Sabbath candlesticks. Later, she moved the hair to the pocket of her apron so it would always be close to her.

The long hair—braided and tied with a red ribbon—remained in her apron pocket through the rest of her journey.

holding onto hope

G abriella was terribly frightened, but she didn't want to show her parents she was afraid.

She asked, "Why are they sending us away? Where are we going?"

Again, she saw her mother cry, and she cried with her.

They could only take a few items with them on their trip to the work camp—things like non- perishable food, sleeping gear, and cooking utensils. Gabriella's father hitched their wagon to two of his favorite horses, and they loaded it with whatever they could carry on their backs. They kept alive a belief that life would become normal again, like the old times. In that way, they held onto hope as they braced themselves for change.

The seven family members rode in a procession with the other Jewish families from their town. The procession traveled twelve miles to a larger town where they were moved into a neighborhood with two streets blocked off. Then they were led to a large lumberyard in this neighborhood. It had a fence all around so no one could escape. The only way to get in or out of this place required special passes.

This neighborhood was called the Jewish ghetto.

Once the family arrived at the ghetto and began removing their possessions from the wagon, Gabriella's father gave his two favorite horses a gentle tap. Then he handed the reins to a local gypsy and said, "Take care of these horses; they're nice animals."

This made a strong impression on Gabriella. Even in these uncertain times, one thing was certain. Her father was a kind-hearted man who loved animals and especially horses.

❀ ❀ ❀ ❀ ❀ ❀

act of kindness

G abriella and her family remained in this Jewish ghetto for two weeks. They were not allowed to leave, and police patrolled the perimeter to make sure they didn't try. They had to live in a single-family home with ten other families and didn't have much food and water. They tried to feel hopeful that their lives would improve once they got to their new home at the work camp.

The family was still together and for this they were grateful.

A kindly Christian neighbor named Elizabeth, who stood barely five feet tall, travelled from their hometown to bring the family food. Because she didn't have a horse and wagon, she made the trip on foot.

Elizabeth adored Gabriella's father because he had always been kind to her, buying whatever butter or cheeses she had for sale, even when he didn't need any. Elizabeth's heart was heavy at the thought of what happened to her Jewish friends, so she walked those miles to bring the family two large loaves of bread, which she carried on her back. She also brought milk for the children. Elizabeth was a kind soul.

Although no one else from their town came to provide food or assistance, Gabriella's family focused on gratitude for Elizabeth's kind efforts rather than the absence of kindness from others. In fact, most of the people in Gabriella's town acted as bystanders. When the Jewish families had to assemble in the town square, some even shouted hateful words.

Their friends and neighbors had turned on them. "How can people do this to one another?" Gabriella thought. She had seen goodness in everyone—until now.

Hate had spread to their little town where families of all faiths had lived together for centuries. Friendships were forgotten because of the awful lies that had been repeated so many times—lies taken as truth.

How could things change so quickly? What had happened to their peaceful community?

hungry and dirty

Simple, joyful thoughts became a distraction for eight-year-old Gabriella, but it was getting harder to feel happy. Seeing stars in the sky at night or birds flying overhead during the day reminded Gabriella of her life back home.

Gabriella had loved her simple home life and wanted it back. She missed the horses, the cow, the chickens, and the geese. She tried to find goodness in her life, appreciating her family and the little they had.

Mostly she was hungry and dirty, and she longed for her bed. She was tired of sleeping on a bare floor.

At her young age, she had learned to recognize exactly what hatred looked like. She wanted to be ready for anything, but everywhere she looked, she saw trouble brewing.

Bad things. Nothing but bad.

transport by freight train

After two weeks of waiting and uncertainty, all the Jewish families in the ghetto were led to the local train station on foot. They were still under the impression they would be dropped off at the work camp, but this time they were led by gendarmes with bayonets.

The families were loaded into freight cars. They had to walk up wooden ramps the soldiers had built to make a smooth transition and avoid panic. But the ramps afforded little comfort when there were soldiers with guns standing on top of the train.

Gabriella's family was led up one of the ramps and corralled into a freight car. The car had two little windows that were covered in barbed wire. This was the only air circulating in the hot and very crowded space.

When the freight car door slammed shut and Gabriella's eyes adjusted to the darkness, she became aware of flies buzzing all around the dirty, cramped space. Body odors came from everywhere.

As the train started to roll, Gabriella and her mother cried. After several hours on the train, a pregnant lady in their freight car gave birth to her baby. The tiny newborn's cries were heard along with wails from others. A teacher from Gabriella's school died in the freight car soon after. Birth and death were happening at the same time in the same cramped, filthy freight car.

Gabriella held tightly to her mother's hand. After three days and three nights, the train finally stopped, and the guards opened the door. They arrived as the sun was almost down and nightfall was approaching. The soldiers were yelling at everyone to get off the train. Amid barking dogs, guards were barking orders in German and pointing with guns to make sure people understood.

But there was no ramp on this side of the car. Strange-looking people with shaved heads wearing dirty striped prison uniforms jumped into the freight car. They pushed people from the train onto the ground—a steep seven-foot drop. As they fell, they landed on top of one another. All their possessions were left at the train station—except for the long hair from Gabriella's haircut. The braid with the red ribbon remained firmly planted in her mother's apron pocket.

The family members lined up and held hands as they walked along a wide concrete pathway. At the end of this wide path stood a tall, impeccably dressed soldier who held a long shepherd's cane. As they got closer, they noticed how the line of people split into two after passing him. The sharply dressed soldier evaluated all of them by their height and physical condition to determine if they would be useful as laborers.

While the other soldiers shouted to keep the line moving, he used his cane to point to where each person should go. "You, to the right. You, to the left." His angry words in German hit the crowd of confused and frightened people like bullets.

no turning back

Ordered by the well-dressed soldier, Gabriella and her twelve-year-old brother went to the left with their mother, who seemed like a shadow of her former self. Gabriella's father looked old and rundown, his handlebar mustache uncombed and messy, his hat crushed from the crowded train and a heavy leather coat flung over his shoulder. After the soldier with the shepherd's cane looked at him, he was also told to go to the left.

Then Gabriella's three teenage brothers were told to go to the right. Instead, the oldest ran to the left to be with his parents. The soldier took his shepherd's cane and grabbed the teenager by his neck, then threw him back to the right with his two brothers.

This happened not once, but twice.

Gabriella stayed by her mother's side the whole time, holding tightly to her hand. They were pushed into the entry way of a bath house, then into a large room of showers. There, they were told to undress and given a small towel and a sliver of soap.

Gabriella closed her eyes and longed for another world, a peaceful life. But there was no turning back.

Epilogue
1998

More than fifty years had passed since Gabriella's haircut.

Audrey felt sad as she went through the treasures her recently deceased mother had left behind. She found a small box on the top shelf of her mother's closet covered with a thick layer of dust. She dusted it off, then opened the box and found a plastic bag holding what looked like a crushed piece of fur.

It took Audrey a minute to figure out what it was: her own long braid from the haircut her mother insisted she get on her twelfth birthday.

Seeing the braid her mother had saved brought back a flood of feelings. This big haircut had been a milestone in Audrey's young life. She closed her eyes as she remembered the events of that day. Among them, she knew she could never forget her mother's pride holding up the long cut-off braid.

Imagine! Her mother had kept the treasured braid in a box on top of her closet **for the rest of her life.**

When Audrey opened her eyes, her sweet childhood memories were replaced with thoughts of Gabriella's haircut and the horrible conditions and circumstances her family had to endure.

She remembered hearing about the haircut from her father and his two brothers—the three teenagers who survived those terrible days together. Their mother's final instruction to her boys was to remind them to always keep the youngest in the middle. If they were to line up to be counted and the line was cut off abruptly, he'd always remain with at least one brother. This mother's loving guidance was her attempt to keep her teenage sons together.

*From the ghetto to the freight car to the large room of showers, Gabriella's mother—Audrey's grandmother—had held onto her daughter's hair. And the treasured braid had remained in her apron pocket **for the rest of her life.***

Reflections

Gabriella's story can teach us about human nature and responsibility for others as we ask these important questions:

- Why did their friends and neighbors turn away from them when they needed help?
- What made Elizabeth risk her life to bring her neighbors food when they were in the Jewish ghetto?
- If you were a neighbor of Gabriella's family, what would you have done?

One thing we know. We can all make a difference for someone else. It begins with kindness.

Author's Note

After years of trying to tell Gabriella's story and struggling to find the right words, I began to transcribe portions of the testimonies my parents and two of my uncles recorded in 1995 for Steven Spielberg's Shoah Foundation. These were my guides to telling Gabriella's story and they revealed a bigger, clearer narrative than I originally anticipated.

My father and two of his brothers provided me with a trio of descriptions of the same events, which gave me a well rounded view of their experiences. I used many of their exact words and descriptions for accuracy of the timelines and conditions.

I've been asked by early readers of this book, "What happened to the three brothers?"

The three teenage brothers remained together through the time they were separated from their parents until their liberation from a labor camp called Bunzlau in southwestern Poland. At the time of their liberation on February 11, 1945, my father had just turned nineteen and his brothers were twenty and seventeen.

The three surviving brothers in 1960, with the youngest brother in the middle.

My father George was the first of the three to emigrate to America, preceding his brothers by a few years. He was also the first to marry and to start a family. Each of the three brothers had two sons and one daughter, and all settled in the Chicago area

My mother had a similar wartime experience, from a town on Hungary's Romanian border. I used portions of her Shoah testimony to provide her innocent perspective of the ghetto and Auschwitz, which gave me some of the words for Gabriella. My mother was liberated on May 5, 1945 from a small women's labor camp called Holysov near the German border in Czechoslovakia. She was sixteen.

Before I could finish writing this book, I had to face my vulnerability and find my own courage.

I grew up surrounded by holocaust survivors, including family, neighbors, and friends. Some were never able to overcome the horrors they witnessed. Some of them just went numb. They had witnessed unimaginable horrors and experienced the worst of man's inhumanity to one another. They survived but didn't speak about their experiences for decades.

When any survivor did openly share a story with me, I was fascinated by the telling moments of kindness during these darkest hours. They looked after each other while sharing food, clothing, or whatever they could to ease someone else's pain.

These moments of kindness were a stark contrast against the backdrop of intense human suffering.

Fortunately for me and my brothers, our parents left us a legacy of love and resilience, although their pain and loss were always under the surface. My lasting impression of my parents is filled with stories about rebuilding their lives triumphantly, their strong will to carry on, and their profound gratitude to America.

I tried to balance the worst in Gabriella's story with a hopeful voice from a sweet eight-year-old girl. It might leave you feeling sad or angry, but it is my intention to also leave you with the hope that future generations will do a better job addressing the issues of intolerance and racism.

USC Shoah Foundation

The Institute for Visual History and Education

The Shoah Foundation was established by Steven Spielberg in 1994 to videotape and preserve interviews with survivors and other witnesses of the holocaust. The foundation moved to its permanent home at the University of Southern California in 2006.

USC Shoah Foundation – The Institute for Visual History and Education develops empathy, understanding and respect through testimony, using its Visual History Archive of more than 55,000 video testimonies, academic programs and partnerships across USC and 175 universities. The award-winning IWitness education program uses these first person stories from survivors to educate, inspire and empower students.

Now in its third decade, USC Shoah Foundation reaches millions of people on six continents from its home at the University of Southern California.

Gabriella's story could not have been told without these valuable testimonies.

About The Author

Audrey Le Roy grew up in the village of Skokie, Illinois, which was home to more than 7000 holocaust survivors.

Currently, she lives in Rancho Mirage, California, with her husband.

In memory of Gabriella, Audrey has kept her hair long her whole life.

the author pictured at age 8, the same age as Gabriella in the story

Acknowledgments

This book has been in my heart for such a long time and I couldn't have completed it without the encouragement, inspiration, friendship and gentle push from many friends and family members. I am deeply indebted to all my early readers who provided me with valuable feedback and never-ending encouragement. Too many names to list. You know who you are.

Heartfelt gratitude to Lynn Price, Kathy Gilbert, Phyllis Riforgiato, and Tom Jakab for playing key roles in helping me fulfill my long held goal of telling Gabriella's story.

Most of all I want to acknowledge my husband Peter, for supporting my goal from start to finish.

Thank you my love, I couldn't have completed this without you.

CPSIA information can be obtained
at www.ICGtesting.com
Printed in the USA
LVHW072143250722
724399LV00005B/40